Maybe Days

A BOOK FOR CHILDREN
IN FOSTER CARE

written by Jennifer Wilgocki, M.S.
and Marcia Kahn Wright, Ph.D.

illustrated by Alissa Imre Geis

MAGINATION PRESS • WASHINGTON, DC

To children in foster care everywhere

To Jim Van Den Brandt, with gratitude — JW

To my parents, and to Erik, Jenny, and Rebecca — MKW

For Mama and Papa — AIG

Published by
M A G I N A T I O N   P R E S S
An Educational Publishing Foundation Book
American Psychological Association
750 First Street, NE
Washington, DC 20002

For more information about our books, including a complete catalog, please write to us,
call 1-800-374-2721, or visit our website at www.maginationpress.com.

Editor: Darcie Conner Johnston
Art Director: Susan K. White
The text type is Bookman.
Printed by Phoenix Color, Rockaway, New Jersey.

Library of Congress Cataloging-in-Publication Data
Wilgocki, Jennifer.
Maybe days : a book for children in foster care / by Jennifer Wilgocki and Marcia Kahn Wright ;
illustrated by Alissa Imre Geis.
p.   cm.
Summary: Introduces the people and procedures involved in foster care, and the feelings, reactions,
and concerns of new foster children. Includes an afterword for caregivers.
ISBN 1-55798-803-X (hc. : alk. paper) — ISBN 1-55798-802-1 (sc. : alk. paper)
1. Foster children — Juvenile literature. 2. Foster home care — Juvenile literature.
[1. Foster home care.]
I. Wright, Marcia Kahn. II. Geis, Alissa Imre, ill. III. Title.
HV881.W54 2002
362.73'3 — dc21
2001045292

Manufactured in the United States of America
10 9 8 7 6 5 4

All kids need a grown-up
to take care of them.

But sometimes, for different reasons, kids can't live with their mom and dad...or just with their mom...or just with their dad. So sometimes kids need to live somewhere else.

That's what this book is about.

Some kids live in a foster home, where grown-ups
called foster parents take care of them.

Living in a foster home is
usually not the kid's idea.

It is also not the kid's fault.

It's not because the kid is
bad or silly or stupid or goofy.

It's because for different
reasons kids sometimes cannot
live with their parents.

Sometimes kids cannot live with their parents because their parents hurt them.

Sometimes kids cannot live with their parents because a parent dies.

Sometimes kids cannot live with their parents because their parents have to be in jail.

Sometimes kids cannot live with their parents because their parents just can't take good enough care of them.

Some kids like their foster parents a lot, even love them.

Some kids have other feelings about their foster parents.

Lots of kids have more than one feeling at the same time.

Some kids get worried if they like their foster parents.

They don't want to hurt anyone's feelings or make anyone sad or mad.

Some kids call their foster parents mom or dad.

Some kids don't.

Some kids don't look much like their foster parents and the people in their new neighborhood.

Some kids look a lot like their foster parents and the people in their new neighborhood.

Sometimes kids and foster parents do a lot of things the same way already. Sometimes there are new things that can be fun and exciting.

Sometimes there is a lot to get used to.
And there is always *something* to get used to.

Sometimes kids and foster parents get along with each other pretty easily.

Sometimes kids and foster parents have troubles they have to work out.

Some kids like to tell people that they live with their foster parents.

Some kids don't like to tell anyone.

They don't like having to explain or answer a million questions or even put up with getting teased.

Foster care can last a short time or a long time.

No matter how long or short it is, kids miss their moms and dads or brothers and sisters or aunts and uncles or pets or friends or neighbors or school or even their bed.

When kids are in foster care they can have big feelings.

Sometimes big feelings turn into troubles like
school troubles, sadness troubles, sleep troubles,
anger troubles, and other troubles.

Sometimes kids need help with their feelings and their
troubles. And there are people who can help.

Foster care involves a lot of people who all do different things.

There are the kids...

And there are a whole lot of grown-ups: the parents, the foster parents, the social worker, the therapist, the lawyers, and the judge.

The grown-ups have different jobs, but one job they all share is making sure kids get taken care of well. And the one thing they all care the most about is the kids.

The parents' job is to learn to solve their own problems and to be good parents.

The foster parents' job is to take good care of the kids.

The social worker's job is to check in with the parents and with the foster parents. The social worker also listens to the kids and helps if there are any problems.

The therapist's job is to help everyone with their big feelings and their troubles and their worries.

The lawyers' job is to speak up for people in court.

The judge's job is to listen to everyone and to have the last say about what will happen and what the plan will be.

The plan depends on the situation.

The judge might say that kids can go home to their parents, or kids can stay in foster care, or kids can get adopted.

Judges also decide if kids can have
visits or kids can't have visits with
their parents and relatives.

Visits can be hard, or visits can be fun,
or visits can be both.

Kids have a lot of different feelings
about visits.

No matter what the judge finally
decides, kids in foster care have to
wait a lot while the grown-ups work
on the plan.

While kids are waiting, they sometimes feel worried or angry or scared
or confused or many other things.

Waiting can be hard.

**When kids ask questions,
the grown-ups often say "maybe."**

Will I go back to my parents? Maybe.

Will I stay with my foster parents? Maybe.

Will I live with my brothers and sisters again? Maybe.

Will I have more visits with my parents? Maybe.

25

It can be hard having so many maybes.

Any day can feel like a maybe day.

Sometimes kids want to hear "yes" or "no"
instead of "maybe."

But kids do the best they can in the middle
of all of the maybes. And even though waiting
can be hard and maybes can be hard, not
everything has to be hard.

A kid's job is always to be a kid.

It is important not to let the waiting and the maybes get in the way of other things like...

going to school, having birthdays, playing with a pet, doing homework, smelling flowers, eating cookies, having friends, riding a bike, following the rules, meeting nice people, running as fast as you can, being good at what you're good at,

and most of all

being
you

There's no maybe about that.

A Note to Foster Parents
And Other Adults

The purpose of this book is to acknowledge the experience of children in foster care: to validate their feelings, to support their coping with uncertainty, to diminish their sense of isolation or aloneness, to decrease their confusion, to lighten any burdens of guilt or fault, to provide opportunities for them to speak about their experiences, to give basic information about the foster care system, and to offer—without false promises—messages that might sustain them.

A TOOL FOR CONVERSATION

This book is a beginning, a platform for conversation. It is meant to be read by a child and an adult together, although over time children may want to re-read it on their own.

Before you and your foster child read this book for the first time, point out that he or she may recognize some aspects of the experiences in this book and not others, while experiences that are very important to him or her may not be mentioned in the book at all. Acknowledging this may help children in your care feel more comfortable talking about their experiences, which in turn will help ease their adjustment.

Each child has his or her own particular pace. Some children may want to read or listen to this book from start to finish; others may need to use the book in a different way. Some children may only be able to absorb a bit at a time. Some may want to skip pages; some may want to read or re-read particular sections but not others.

Make things mentionable. Ideally, children will tell their own stories about foster care, their own feelings, and their own reactions. Be prepared to hear things that are painful, and strive to maintain a tone and attitude that are supportive, truthful, and matter-of-fact. Keep in mind that you cannot fix every complexity faced by children in foster care. Sometimes children will have questions to which the honest answer is "maybe" or "I don't know." If additional information might be available, let the child know what you will do to pursue that information.

Give permission. Even if you have already given the child permission to talk with you about anything, reading this book provides yet another opportunity for you to say:

- It is okay to talk about any aspect of foster care and to ask me any question.
- We do not have to see things exactly the same way.
- I will try to do a good job of listening.
- You can talk about the parts that are sad or bad as well as the good parts.
- You can always talk to me.
- You can also talk to your social worker and your therapist.

If the child is seeing a therapist, you might find it helpful to inform the therapist that you are reading this book with the child.

CHILDREN'S REACTIONS

The enormity of adjustment that children in foster care are asked to make is hard to overstate. Children in foster care may experience and express a range of feelings, many of which may emerge during the reading of this book. Multiple feelings may occur at the same time and may include:

- **Relief and a sense of safety**
  Foster care can be a relief to children. Sometimes this is relief from actual danger; sometimes it offers a reprieve from worry or other stresses.
- **Happiness and a sense of enjoyment**
  At its best, foster care encourages children to develop into their best selves and to enjoy being children. They may feel an increase in pleasure and joy.
- **Sadness**
  Children may be sad about not living with their family members or about whatever events led up to their placement. They may be particularly sad before, during, or after visits with family members.

- **Anger**

  Children may be angry at their parents; they also may be angry at social workers or other adults whom they see as responsible for their placement. This anger is often expressed in the foster home.

- **Fear or worry**

  Children have many worries about family members left behind or from whom they have been separated. They may worry about parents, for example, even if they are also angry at those parents. Children may also have many fears about what will happen to them and what the plan for their future will be.

- **Confusion**

  Children in foster care often have misunderstandings or misperceptions about the legal process and plans as well as adult matters that led to their placement. They may also be confused about the adults' roles and decision-making powers.

- **Guilt**

  One of the most common issues among children in foster care is self-blame. They may feel a sense of responsibility even if they understand the reasons for their placement.

- **Shame**

  Children may feel a sense of shame about the simple fact of being in foster care.

- **Loneliness**

  Children may feel lonely in response to missing particular people or places. They may also feel alone or set apart in their status as foster children. Sometimes cultural differences between children and their foster families contribute to a sense of loneliness.

- **Sense of loss**

  Children in foster care endure tremendous loss. They may grieve the loss of people, places, possessions, or everything familiar to them. Even if foster care provides relief or a reprieve from abuse, it always involves some kind of loss as well.

Some children respond well to verbal discussion about their feelings. Foster parents can use "wondering" statements such as, "I wonder how you felt when you first came here." Other helpful questions might include, "What is one thing you really miss?" or "What is one thing you like about the way we do things here?" Children may also want to use pictures rather than words to express themselves, and choose to draw their own pictures in response to parts of this book. You might ask or suggest: "Draw a picture of one thing you miss." "Can you draw a picture of your old friends and your family?" "Draw one thing that makes you happy." "Would you like to draw a picture of the thing you are worried about the most?"

Keep in mind that asking questions and encouraging activities can be useful for some children, but it is not always necessary and is never a substitute for simply listening.

CHANGES OF PLACEMENT

Some children have lived in more than one foster home or experienced multiple moves, and some children's placements have included group homes, kinship placements, and other arrangements. Although such experiences are not directly addressed in this book, it is important for foster parents to address them.

Children who have experienced multiple moves may need to talk about their various placements, the losses involved in their moves, and their perceptions concerning the reasons for their moves. The issue of self-blame may arise in this context, and social workers and other professionals may be of assistance in helping the child sort out reasons for changes in placement. These adults may be able to convey information that helps the child understand that he or she is not to blame. Foster parents can help further by encouraging children to tell stories about their previous placements, draw pictures of places where they have lived (e.g., a map of moves), or share photographs or other memories.

CULTURAL ISSUES AND OTHER DIMENSIONS OF DIFFERENCE

Children and foster families can discover many dimensions of difference, including but not limited to race, class, religion, and family constellation. It is essential that children be encouraged to verbalize thoughts and feelings about any differences. This book provides an opportunity to acknowledge them. Open and matter-of-fact discussion about such issues as religious differences, differences in skin color or in the care of hair and skin, or differences in holiday celebrations prevents these issues from becoming unmentionable and may diminish feelings of discomfort, worry, and loneliness. For example, ask your child about his or her traditions, or encourage him or her to draw pictures of remembered rituals and celebrations.

COMPLEXITIES AND CHALLENGES

Some aspects of foster care present particular challenges for foster parents as well as dilemmas for foster children.

- **Complicated loyalties**

  Children often feel torn between loyalty to their biological families and loyalty to their foster families, regardless of the circumstances of their situation. Give children the message that it is all right to care for and care about many people at the same time. Children often need assistance negotiating this issue, as well as permission to talk about it directly.

- **Visitations**

  Arrangements regarding visitation vary greatly, but for many children visits with parents and other family members can stir up a mix of strong emotions and reactive behaviors. This is one arena where loyalty conflicts can be felt acutely by the child. Anxieties and worries may intensify around visits, although it is also true that visits can be reassuring for children. Reactions can occur in anticipation of visits and following visits, as well as during the visits themselves. Again, direct discussion between child and foster parent can be of help. Offer invitations for discussion, and follow the child's lead. Social workers and therapists can also be helpful in such discussions with the child.

- **Blame, fault, and responsibility**

  Foster care can elicit a tendency to blame: blaming children for their behavior, blaming birth parents for their actions or circumstances, blaming the courts for their decisions, blaming social workers for their man-agement, blaming foster parents for their child-rearing strategies, and so on. This book provides an opportunity for you to shift the conversation away from issues of blame and fault toward issues of accountability and responsibility.

  For example, it can help you convey that being in foster care is not the child's fault but that everyone, the child included, remains responsible for their own actions. Similarly, if appropriate, you may discuss the problems faced by the child's birth parents honestly, without blaming the birth parents, and in a manner that does not intensify the child's conflicts of loyalty. If issues of blame and fault are particularly difficult or loom large for a child, it can be especially helpful to involve social workers and therapists in these discussions.

HELP IS AVAILABLE

Emphasize to children the central fact that many adults care about them and can provide them with help and support as they navigate their foster care experiences. Above all, children in foster care (as all children) need to know that they are not alone.

Help is also available to foster parents. Sometimes direct consultation between parents and professionals is the most useful. At other times, foster parents and foster children can participate together in a therapeutic process. This is a decision that can be made by foster parents and therapists together.

FINAL WORD

For some children, foster care is a brief interruption. For many others, it is a long process that can last for years. Regardless of their circumstances, children in foster care need support and resources, and above all they need to be helped to find ways to live full lives and to become fully themselves.

Foster parenting can be a great challenge. It is always of great importance. Foster parents and other adults can play a vital role in the life of a child. May children thrive in your care.